IGNORANT
AND
AGNOSTIC

IGNORANT
AND
AGNOSTIC

Poems and Other Words

By Stuart Eric Card

STUART CARD PUBLISHING

This is a work of fiction. Names, characters, places, and incidents either are the product of the author's imagination or are used fictitiously, and any resemblance to actual persons, living or dead, business establishments, events, or locales is entirely coincidental.

Cover illustration "Brodrick: The Cool Hat" by Stuart Edward Card © 2008.

ISBN 978-0-615-25664-1

Library of Congress Control Number: 2008909317

*This book is dedicated
To the love of my life,
Joanie Morgan Card.*

*A special thanks to my father,
Stuart Edward Card,
For the incredible
Front cover.*

CONTENTS

I.

IGNORANT

The Jack of No Trades

The Jack of no trades,
The Jack of spades.
With whiskey on his breath,
He awaits his death,
And everything after.

His smile is gray. His teeth are yellow.
His solitude sacrifices sons and fellow.

No Jill to warm his transient bed
While whispers warp his wintered head.

Gesturing, joking, jeering . . .
We all live in vain.
No matter how unlucky,
Or how insane,
Life will always breathe at least a little rain.

Hip-hop Hopscotch

This boy he loved.
He loved and he tried.

Hip-hop hopscotch
Dancing in the daylight's bliss.

Miles of dotted lines
On thick fresh tar
Burning his tires, his nose,
And pushing the pedal with his toes.

Away he drives
From what he will still arrive.
Mediocrity: land of the damned.

"Suicide Lullaby," the radio replied.

He laughs, he cries,
He works, he sighs,
He breathes, he tries,
He putts, he drives.

But damned to the road
He forever drives.
Fills his tank with fuel of pride.
Achieving once, what once was won.

Hip-hop hopscotch
Burning scars on his broken fists.

More roads tomorrow.
More soda for sorrow.
He wakes for hope,
Of which he will only borrow.

Born of Savages

I was born of savages
Of the down-trodden
Of the lost

I ached for the life of the refined
The distinguished
The aristocrat

As my legs grew long
Like my hapless beard
I longed for a life with you

Who am I to ask of you your life
Your time
Your death

My savage heart rages beneath this vested suit
This collared mockery
This silk lie

The anger at this pointless joke
This wheel-spinning
This circus

Broken on the thought that my great is never good
Never par
Never fine

Sullen knowledge of my fraud
Of my guise
Of my life

If not for a few who bear witness to this cheat
And convince me it divine
I'd lay rest to it all
And bed everlasting in the shadow of the tall.

Ain't Takin' Me

The train for the future comes
Stops at the station
They're takin' tickets
But they ain't takin' mine

(CHORUS)

They won't take me
Ain't takin' me
Ain't takin' me

Standing at the station
The last train has gone
My baggage is my pride
And it fits in a small bag

Don't matter no how
'Cause they got no more room
I can see that ain't true
And that just won't do

(CHORUS)

They won't take me
Ain't takin' me
Ain't takin' me

A new line comes
But it turns at the corner
Back to the first stop
A round trip it seems

(CHORUS)

They won't take me
Ain't takin' me
Ain't takin' me

No Sound of Evil

He awakes in a place where there lives no sound of evil, no vein of strain, no loss of joy. He sleeps far from that place; no stars to calm, no light to sooth, and nothing to lose. Yet when dawn comes life springs through his veins and the night is lost.

And when he is away, the water still drips to that comforting rhythm. Every plant still breathes the day's warm air. Every corner still acquires its daily dose of dust. But something is changing there by the minute, and he is beginning to grow an escalating dislike for it.

He performs his nightly ritual of taunting the night sky; "No moon shine can out-shine my moonshine." To which the night sky replies: "How lonely are you tonight?" That is when the inside of the bottle gets closer to being empty and dry like the inside of his mouth will be come the morn.

What change bathes in his empty bath? Who haunts and taunts him where no one exists but he? In the end he sees that he has created through destruction the imperishable monster that perches over him at night. Doubt. Failure. Hopelessness. Loneliness.

Full-Length Wool Coats

In the winter months
When the gavel-dancers prance around those old oak halls
In their full-length wool coats.
Convincing courts with charismatic cool,
With words that bounce and flounce with glee
Within the wooden-hammer school,
And in their full-length wool coats.

Their pride, their arrogance, their justified swagger
Accentuated by the swoosh and flutter of
Their full-length wool coats.
The tan, the black, the charcoal, the blue shapes of those coats:
So slender at parts, so chunky at others;
Those full-length wool coats.

Watch them bop and watch them tap:
So graceful, so beautiful, so rushed,
But mostly so shameful
In their full-length wool coats.

Tops of My Shoes

Tops of my shoes: worn and educated leather.
Laces in absurdly neat bows
Juxtaposed against tattered, unhealthy jeans
And even that against a shirt with button holes sewn together,
Pinned together by hope and misery.

Harmonizing footsteps
In synchronicity with the street tempo.
Rough, rustic, even religious in ways are the tops of my shoes
Considering wooden bridges they've kicked, or
Walls they've rested their tired ends.

Depressed by diffident streets.
Done and dead in many ways, fresh and jive in others.
Served their simple purpose in a sort of trepid dignity.
Puddles, peddles, and pedals alike
Suffer the same turpitude when placed unconcerned under my
soles.

To see the tops of my shoes
To see what used to shine, what used to sate every pedal desire.
And then to see the ill, weak but tumultuous remains.
But these are the tops of my shoes;
The ones I know; the ones that got me from there to here.
If I never look up again . . . life could be worse.

That Ghost and I

That Ghost and I,
We are just friends.
That spider and I,
We are just neighbors.
That corner and I,
We are just empty.
Reality and I,
We have just met.

That Ghost and I,
We are just friends.
That tree and I,
We are just laughing.
That bench and I,
We are just scared.
Truth and I,
We are just lonely.

My Ignorance

Burnt to the paper that reached for me
Scorched to the pen that saw
Screaming to the hell that bore your name
Blinding in the eyes of the law

Never cease to ignore reason and thought
What glacier of truth no one has brought
Snow covered lies; belief only sought

Forgive me
So blunt is my tongue
So blatant is my voice
My boorish ignorance
Is my only choice

I lobbied my duplicity
I fought for your mind
And adopted Oedipus
As the first of my kind

I I.

AND

A Box

A box
A fancy box
Soaked faces
Painted face
One's completion
One's launch
Final words
Deaf ears
Reflection
Redirection
To be earthed
To be unbound
Half-opened box
Closed box
An unlit box
A Forever Box

Where'd Yesterday Go

(CHORUS)

Make your memory fade away.
And make my day.
Tomorrow will be the day you said
"Where'd yesterday go?"

I know tomorrow will always be a brighter day.
She said "it's gonna rain, might as well be today."
Gonna make you cry. Gonna make you insane.
But only if you let them win, so make your play.

(CHORUS)

Make your memory fade away.
And make my day.
Tomorrow will be the day you said
"Where'd yesterday go?"

No one knows the reason why you wanna stay away:
Breakin' the curse you placed . . .
You placed on layaway.
Seconds away from sorrow,
But instead you decide to play
And make the best of waking every day.

(CHORUS)

Make your memory fade away.
And make my day.
Tomorrow will be the day you said
"Where'd yesterday go?"

Wrought Iron Gates

We often pass those wrought iron gates.
The ones that enclose the things we crave,
And the things we hate.

Hinges: rusted; unlocked.
And we stare and we wait.
Too afraid to breach
What we can't even contemplate.

The friction is immense,
And the anxiety is great.
You know now, what I knew all along:
Some things are chance,
But this fate.

And I have walked in the woods where the greatest grizzly
crawls.
But no matter how hard I try and no matter how often rain
falls,
With all the sympathy I do create in those old wooden
walls,
I can't open the gate to the memories in those
halls.

Lawful Lies

Lawful lies; they don't lie anymore.
Tears of joy; they don't cry anymore.

But life is just the same when you're four,
'Cause tomorrow always comes as before.

Symphony of light at your door.
Even so, you tend to ignore.

She never treated life as a chore,
But I'll never see her face anymore.

Time is the mother of all whores:
Raped, beaten and left on the floor.

Running backwards through a field of corn.
Backwards; life runs to the core.

Next to light, life is a bore.
Tomorrow always comes as before.

The Bottle

Here is to you!
As I drop to a knee
And then to another.
I approach the floor,
For I am no brother.

My tongue is rage.
My heart . . . a pacifier.
As I spin the bottle
And light the fire.

Another bottle is open.
Another bottle is empty.
And I fall,
And fall,
Far below what I had fallen before.

The trees sigh.
The fire screams.
The bottle is heavy,
Or as life, it seems.

So, here is to you,
My family at hand.
Those who breathe,
Shan't forget those who can't.

The College Salute

Onwards to the shore of drunken stupidity.
Onwards to the land of laughter and insanity.
Be still not your heart . . .
Pound! Pound! Pound!
And be my brother tonight.

And if you drink,
Drink one for me and then yourself.
Drink another and another,
And lay your glass to the shelf.
Drink 'til you're drunk for sure,
And then drink one more.

May the clock be silent tonight,
In the hopes I lose my sight.
For I drank for you, and I can have no more,
So bottoms up
(I hope you score).

Lastly, I pray for more merry moment.
Shall we keep this night dear.
Remember love, not to fear,
And be young, young, young.
Tonight is for you, I and plenty of beers.
So drink one more with me.
Cheers!

Brodrick, Part One

He will cry and fight,
Lie and bleed.

He will sing.

He will face hate and fight hunger,
Lose sleep and lack focus.

He will laugh.

He will scar and ache,
Cheat and lose.

He will live.

He will seek the middle,
But burn both ends.

He will love.

He will know the bottom and abandon pride,
Fall away and run from.

He will rise.

He will learn little from me,
Less from others.

He will teach.

He will be Brodrick,
And he will save me.
My beautiful son.

So Young

Got a bucket of problems
And no one to solve them

Don't forget my name

No one remembers
Who we fell for

Don't forget my name

(CHORUS)

I know we are
Oh, so young
Oh, so young

Come on and bring it
You know I got it

Till the morning comes

You know I have
As much patience as

A bucket of rum

(CHORUS)

I know we are
Oh, so young
Oh, so young

Brodrick, Part Two

Last night I sat at his crib-side
Alone in the dark I cried
I cried hard
I cried long

"I am your Judas"
I whispered carefully
"And I have betrayed you"

I loved him
And love him still
But where once he had my all
Soon he will suffer my half

My Beautiful Selfish Life

The selfish life I lead
Where your misfortune
Becomes the recognition
Of my good deed

And in my selfish life
The world is cruel
And people unkind
Only in private strife

I will help the needy
I will feed the poor
'Cause of that satisfaction
I am greedy

I will make you smile
I will make it a better day
Not 'cause you're worth it
'Cause I am by a mile

In my beautiful selfish life
The world revolves around me
As long as I let it . . .
And get permission from my wife.

Morgan, Part One

What goes for one goes double for you
You're not the first
You'll never be number two

Mistakes I've made no less than thrice
Shall impart onto you
As Wisdom's price

As you grow our family to four
Like he before
You, we adore

Bring with you what you will
You're sure to best our hopes
And carry us tall
Through the valleys and the slopes

Years will pass ever faster
Be certain to embrace you
And the waves of life you'll master

A Conversation with My Pen

Write! Damn you, write!
Spill from me a story or antidote.
Dispel these dreary 'discomfortable' days.
Follow the compulsion or revulsion that
Causes such words to tap on your tongue
And quibble with your mind and thought.
Throw yourself in with the lions or house cats
(whichever frighten you more)
And come out with wisdom and truth, and tales, and tails.
Remind me of why this or anything else
Makes sense or even should.

"Why is this damn ink never satisfied"
      (Perpetually bruising my finger, my mind, me).
"Leave me alone and let me be,"
      (My words only go so far, only mean so much,
      And I can only go so far, do so much).
"Damn stubborn ink,"
      (It will never dry, it will never cause me to think,
      But will continue to drive me to the edge, forcing me
      to sink).

Stop whining!
Stop trying to counter what cannot be countered,
And craft me some crescendo that conquers catastrophe.
Sell me your spirit of sin, sacrifice, or splendor,
And tell me a moral, or
Teach me the way.

"If I knew I would.
But when the ink flows from your belly,
I'm not completely sure it's my morals that speak.
I'm not certain at all of what I think . . .
If that is indeed what I am doing."

Stop procrastinating!
Exaggerate, fascinate, and force me to contemplate.
I will accept no excuse, and I expect written abuse.
Feed me lies, feed me what you will.
I don't care and probably never will.
As long as you write. DAMN YOU, WRITE!

She-Kah-Go

She can go, She-kah-go
Sky is scraped
And wind is shaped
By She-kah-go

She can go, She-kah-go
Tongues have tasted
And no steak is wasted
In She-kah-go

She can go, She-kah-go
Bears soldier the field
But cubs ivied their shield
In She-kah-go

She can go, She-kah-go
Magnificent is the mile
And tender is the smile
In She-kah-go

She can go, She-kah-go
A good man plays
Though winter stays
In She-kah-go

She can go, She-kah-go
Parks made of wicker
And children less sicker
In She-kah-go

She can go, She-kah-go
The lake blows a kiss
And she will miss
She-kah-go

The Thistle That Spilt My Blood

The thistle that spilt my blood
Upon the rusted soil,
Healed my poisoned wounds.

Ever since,
I hear the cry of the thistle in the somber mist
By her deadly seas and ancient peaks,
For her slaughtered castles,
Her defiant and broken people,
And for me – her lost son.

My blood will forever bleed tartan,
And my spit will forever thirst cold northern waters,
But she is almost certain to never be my home,
And so we weep together.

St. Andrews' haunted ruins will never be my neighbor,
Nor will I perpetually wake in Aberdeen,
Or raise my children on Princess Street.
No, the blood she spilt is the only part of me she'll have
And so we weep together.

The thistle that spilt my blood
Upon the rusted soil,
Cries to me in my sleep,
And insures that as long as I am not there,
I am always nowhere.

III.

AGNOSTIC

Rebirth

I have death-ed,
And liv-ed once more.
As have we all,
And all the more.

So I claim:
God be known,
And know me more!

A guide I lack.
But I travel more.
The pain of life.
The harm of loving more.

Die I may.
I have done it before.
But live I must,
At least once more.

The Haunting

I'm haunted by what I did not see,
And what I did not see coming.
The creeping, the crazy,
And the crystallitic images that were never there.

Who be?
Or worse, who not be there?

The words that twist and wrench the empty vestibules
Of what I can only assume used to be . . .
Filled.

The vacant hallways, the crooked stairs, the ripped carpet.
And no one was there.
No one was there to say "boo!"
No one was there to chase that demon that dwells in that place;
That place that I go when I see what I did not see.

Say "boo." SAY "BOO!!!"
Somebody say what needs to be said
And scare that demon until he is dead.

Did you see?
Or are you as lost as me?

I cannot prove that He is not right there.
Or who He is.
Or if I care.
But I cannot look,
I'm afraid to stare.
I cannot force myself to see what is not there.

Agnosticism

No one remembers how it started
      And no one's left to say:
"There's nobody out there takin' notice
      That there's no one left to pay!
      That there's no one left to pay!"

Burning my bridges of salvation.
      There's gonna be hell to pay.
Searching my soul for an excuse to say:
      That God's the only way.
      That God's the only way.

Battle everyday with no devotion,
      Only one thing to say:
Can't break free from the institutions
      That run my everyday.
      That run my everyday.

(CHORUS)

Break the cycle, break the cycle
      And think for yourself.
Break the cycle, break the cycle
      And think for yourself.

Always singing songs of glory,
      But only on Sunday.
Problem comes on Monday morning
      When reality says no way.
      When reality says no way.

Never questionin' or nothin'
      Gotta follow what they say.
Small minds, for small people,
      Just following what they say.
      Just following what they say.

(CHORUS)

Break the cycle, break the cycle
      And think for yourself.
Break the cycle, break the cycle
      And think for yourself.

Listen

Carrying the burden further
To destination: Unfound
With sparks of laughter and purity
Of the children we once knew

And losing something we can't see
And playing with something we can't feel
Crying over your buried fate
Testing what you know to be true

This, That, and The Other

This whisper I seek
This faded canon
This broken whole
This blunted talon

That I know less now
That I once was fond
That all is lost
That all I had is gone

The other I almost knew
The other I imagine
The other is true
The other is fashion

A Piece of Peace

A piece of peace
A rested soul
The search un-ceased
A travel: none toll

Forever we pass
The Forgotten Tree
Passioned by grass
And standing so free

The Brilliant Crest
By its founding sea
Within my chest
I found me

A Choice

Of kings and queens
And old blue jeans
I crossed a path of crossed crosses.
I never knew the new news
Until that day I knew.

And for all of you
Who choose to choose:
Never walk on walks walking.
Run, I run to run, run.

Die I shall in graceful peace
Like geese on a winter passing.
But I think to think of a thought I thought . . .
To never die standing.